Hit The Mark

Achieve Your Goals

Goals Planner
with coloring pages
DeAnna Troupe

ISBN: 978-0-359-32834-5

"People with goals succeed because they know where they're going." - **Earl Nightingale**

JANUARY

MONTHLY GOALS

Tasks required to achieve goals

Obstacles I Might Face & How I Will Overcome Them

Weekly Progress

JANUARY

WEEK 1

JANUARY

WEEK 2

JANUARY

WEEK 3

JANUARY

WEEK 4

JANUARY

WEEK 5

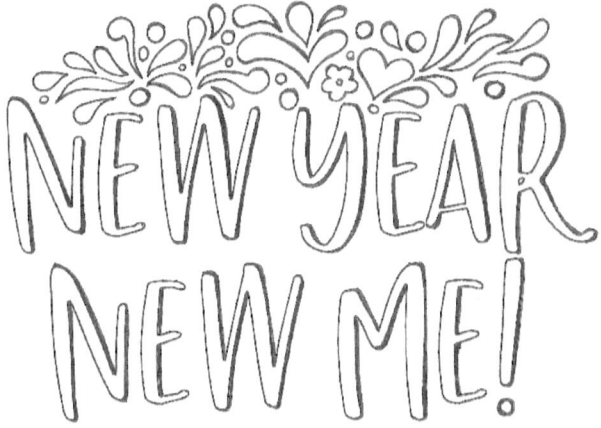

Goals allow you to control the direction of change in your favor. -Brian Tracy

FEBRUARY

Weekly Progress
February

WEEK 1

February

WEEK 2

February

WEEK 3

February

WEEK 4

LOVE IS ALL AROUND ME

"Set your goals high, and don't stop till you get there."
- Bo Jackson

MARCH

MONTHLY GOALS

Tasks required to achieve goals

Obstacles I Might Face & How I Will Overcome Them

Weekly Progress

MARCH

WEEK 1

MARCH

WEEK 2

MARCH

WEEK 3

MARCH

WEEK 4

MARCH

WEEK 5

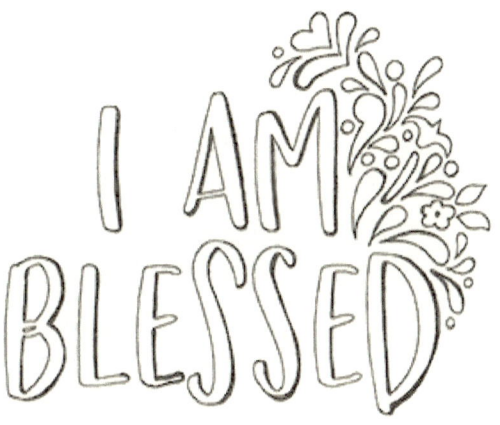

"Discipline is the bridge between goals and accomplishment." - Jim Rohn

April

MONTHLY GOALS

Tasks required to achieve goals

Obstacles I Might Face & How I Will Overcome Them

Weekly Progress

April

WEEK 1

April

WEEK 2

April

WEEK 3

April

WEEK 4

April

WEEK 5

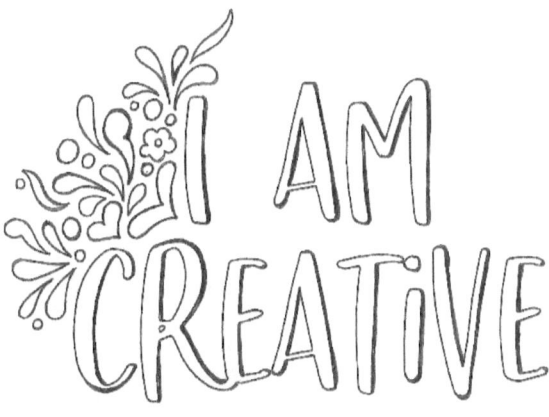

"When it is obvious that the goals cannot be reached, don't adjust the goals, adjust the action steps." - **Confucius**

May

MONTHLY GOALS

Tasks required to achieve goals

Obstacles I Might Face & How I Will Overcome Them

Weekly Progress

May

WEEK 1

May

WEEK 2

May

WEEK 3

May

WEEK 4

May

WEEK 5

I AM MOVING FORWARD!

"One way to keep momentum going is to have constantly greater goals." - Michael Korda

June

MONTHLY GOALS

Tasks required to achieve goals

Obstacles I Might Face & How I Will Overcome Them

Weekly Progress

June

WEEK 1

June

WEEK 2

June

WEEK 3

June

WEEK 4

June

WEEK 5

I CHOOSE LOVE TODAY

"Review your goals twice every day in order to be focused on achieving them." - Les Brown

July

MONTHLY GOALS

Tasks required to achieve goals

Obstacles I Might Face & How I Will Overcome Them

Weekly Progress

July

WEEK 1

July

WEEK 2

July

WEEK 3

July

WEEK 4

July

WEEK 5

I EMBRACE EASE & FLOW

"What keeps me going is goals." - Muhammad Ali

August

MONTHLY GOALS

Tasks required to achieve goals

Obstacles I Might Face & How I Will Overcome Them

Weekly Progress

August

WEEK 1

August

WEEK 2

August

WEEK 3

August

WEEK 4

August

WEEK 5

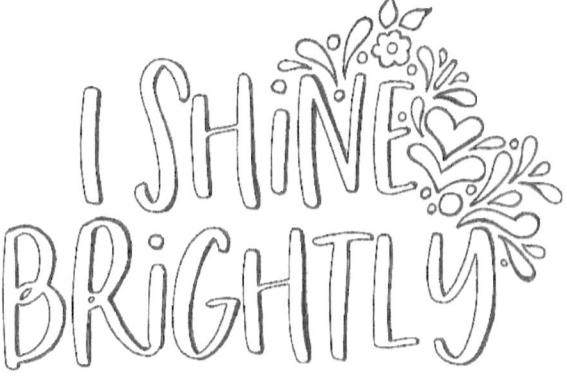

I don't focus on what I'm up against. I focus on my goals and I try to ignore the rest.
-Venus Williams

September

MONTHLY GOALS

Tasks required to achieve goals

Obstacles I Might Face & How I Will Overcome Them

Weekly Progress

September

WEEK 1

September

WEEK 2

September

WEEK 3

September

WEEK 4

September

WEEK 5

LEAN IN TO YOUR DREAM!

"Goals transform a random walk into a chase."

- Mihaly Csikszentmihalyi

October

MONTHLY GOALS

Tasks required to achieve goals

Obstacles I Might Face & How I Will Overcome Them

Weekly Progress

October

WEEK 1

October

WEEK 2

October

WEEK 3

October

WEEK 4

October

WEEK 5

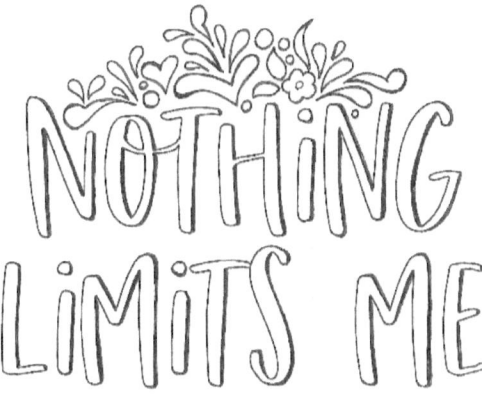

"I think goals should never be easy, they should force you to work, even if they are uncomfortable at the time."

- Michael Phelps

November

MONTHLY GOALS

Tasks required to achieve goals

Obstacles I Might Face & How I Will Overcome Them

Weekly Progress

November

WEEK 1

November

WEEK 2

November

WEEK 3

November

WEEK 4

November

WEEK 5

TOGETHER
WE RISE

"The motivation is in my heart to work toward my goals and my dreams." - Nonito Donaire

December

MONTHLY GOALS

Tasks required to achieve goals

Obstacles I Might Face & How I Will Overcome Them

Weekly Progress

December

WEEK 1

December

WEEK 2

December

WEEK 3

December

WEEK 4

December

WEEK 5

MY LiFE iS MY GiFT

(this page intentionally left blank)

(this page intentionally left blank)

Other coloring books by DeAnna
Troupe

Drawing A Blank: An Adult
Coloring Book With Mandalas For
Relaxation And Stress Relief